The Path to Positivity

Overcoming Negativity and Embracing Happiness

PRADIP N DAS

implied. Readers acknowledge that the author is not engaging in the rendering of legal, financial, medical or professional advice. The content within this book has been derived from various sources. Please consult a licensed professional before attempting any techniques outlined in this book.

By reading this document, the reader agrees that under no circumstances is the author responsible for any losses, direct or indirect, which are incurred as a result of the use of information contained within this document, including, but not limited to, — errors, omissions, or inaccuracies.

Table of Contents

Table of Contents 1

Introduction 5

Understanding Negativity 21

The Power of Positive Thinking 40

Overcoming Negativity 56

Embracing Happiness 72

Putting it into Practice...............................93

Action Points 112

Conclusion 115

Introduction

Michael Phelps, widely regarded as one of the greatest swimmers of all time, is not only known for his incredible athletic achievements but also for his remarkable resilience and positive mindset. Throughout his career, Phelps faced numerous challenges, from injuries to personal struggles. However, he never let these obstacles stop him from pursuing his dreams.

One of Phelps' most iconic moments came at the 2008 Beijing Olympics, where he won eight gold medals in a single games. However, this incredible feat was not achieved without facing significant adversity. In the lead-up to the Olympics, Phelps' coach was suspended, and he had to work with a new coach in a new training environment. Despite the challenges, Phelps remained focused and optimistic, working harder than ever before to achieve his goals.

David Beckham, one of the most famous footballers of all time, is known not just for his impressive athletic ability, but also for his positive attitude both on and off the field. Throughout his career, Beckham has faced countless challenges and setbacks - from being dismissed from the England team after receiving a red card in the 1998 World Cup, to sustaining a career-threatening injury while playing for AC Milan in 2010.

Despite these difficulties, Beckham remained unwaveringly positive, always focusing on the opportunities and possibilities that lay ahead. He once said, "I'm a positive person. I always think of the best possible scenarios." This positivity not only helped him overcome his setbacks, but also served as an inspiration to those around him.

Garry Kasparov, widely considered to be one of the greatest chess players of all time, is known not just for his incredible talent, but also for his unwavering positive attitude both on and off the board. Throughout his career, Kasparov faced countless challenges - from fierce competition to political pressure - but he never let these obstacles dampen his spirit. One of Kasparov's most famous matches was against the IBM computer Deep Blue in 1997. After winning the first match, Kasparov lost the second and was left feeling frustrated and defeated. However, rather than giving up, he used this setback as motivation to push harder and come back stronger. In the end, Kasparov won the match and proved once again that his positive mindset was an essential part of his success.

With 20 Grand Slam titles and countless other achievements, Roger Federer's success on the court has made him a true icon of the sport. Throughout his career, Federer has faced his share of challenges. He has dealt with injuries, tough losses, and the pressure of constantly being in the spotlight. Yet through it all, he has remained remarkably positive, always focusing on the opportunities and possibilities in front of him rather than dwelling on the negatives.

One of the most powerful examples of Federer's positivity came in 2016, when he was forced to take six months off from the sport due to injury. Rather than letting this setback get him down, Federer used the time to focus on his mental and physical well-being, taking up yoga and spending more time with his family.

When he returned to the court, Federer was refreshed and revitalized, and went on to have one of the most successful seasons of his career, winning two Grand Slam titles and regaining his place at the top of the rankings.

The story of Phelps', Beckham, Kasparav and Federer are the examples of the incredible power of positivity in our lives. When we approach difficulties with a positive attitude, we are more resilient, more creative, and more open to new possibilities. We are able to find the strength and determination to keep pushing forward, no matter what obstacles may arise.

In this book, we will explore the ways in which it can transform our lives. We will look at real-life examples of individuals who have overcome adversity and found success through embracing positivity, and we will provide practical strategies for cultivating a positive mindset in our own lives. If you are looking to live a happier, more fulfilling life, this book will offer valuable insights and guidance on your journey.

Overcoming Negativity and Embracing Happiness" aims to provide readers with an understanding of the importance of a positive mindset, the impact of negativity on our lives, and the benefits of embracing positivity.

We live in a world that is full of challenges and obstacles, and it is easy to get caught up in negative thinking and emotions. Negative self-talk, self-doubt, and a lack of confidence can hold us back from achieving our goals and living a fulfilling life. Furthermore, chronic negativity can lead to stress, anxiety, and depression, impacting both our mental and physical health.

On the other hand, a positive mindset can lead to greater resilience, optimism, and happiness. Positive thinking can help us to see opportunities instead of obstacles, approach challenges with a growth mindset, and build stronger relationships with others.

"The Path to Positivity" is designed to help readers understand the psychology behind negativity, identify negative thought patterns, and learn practical strategies for cultivating a positive mindset. By building resilience and optimism, readers will be able to overcome setbacks and failures, cope with stress and anxiety, and find greater meaning and purpose in their lives.

Through a combination of scientific research, psychological insights, and practical exercises, this book aims to empower readers to take control of their thinking and emotions, and embrace positivity as a way of life. The path to positivity is not always easy, but by learning to challenge negative self-talk, build resilience, and cultivate gratitude and mindfulness, readers will be on their way to a happier, healthier, and more fulfilling life.

The importance of a positive mindset

A positive mindset is essential for achieving personal growth, success, and happiness. It allows us to approach challenges and obstacles with a growth mindset, focusing on the opportunities instead of the barriers. When we have a positive mindset, we are more likely to feel optimistic about the future, have higher self-esteem, and experience greater overall well-being.

Studies have shown that having a positive mindset can lead to a range of benefits, including reduced stress and anxiety, improved physical health, and better coping skills. A positive mindset can also help us to build stronger relationships with others, as we are more likely to approach others with empathy, compassion, and kindness.

On the other hand, a negative mindset can hold us back from achieving our goals and living a fulfilling life. Negative self-talk, self-doubt, and a lack of confidence can lead to feelings of anxiety, depression, and low self-esteem. Chronic negativity can also lead to physical health problems, as stress and anxiety can impact our immune system, cardiovascular health, and overall well-being.

Learning to cultivate a positive mindset is not always easy, but it is a crucial step towards achieving personal growth and happiness. By focusing on the positive aspects of our lives, challenging negative thought patterns, and practicing gratitude and mindfulness, we can develop a more positive outlook on life and experience greater overall well-being.

The impact of negativity on our lives

Negativity can have a profound impact on our lives, affecting our emotional, physical, and mental well-being. Negative thinking can lead to feelings of anxiety, stress, and depression, which can impact our relationships, work, and overall quality of life. In this article, we will explore the impact of negativity on our lives and provide some strategies for overcoming negative thinking patterns.

Negative thinking can have a ripple effect on our lives, impacting not only our thoughts and emotions but also our behavior and physical health. When we engage in negative self-talk or ruminate on our problems, we can become stuck in a cycle of negativity, which can impact our daily life in a number of ways.

One of the most significant impacts of negativity is on our emotional well-being. Negative thinking can lead to feelings of sadness, anger, and frustration, which can make it difficult to enjoy life and connect with others. Negative thinking can also lead to feelings of low self-esteem, self-doubt, and shame, which can impact our relationships with others and our overall quality of life.

Another significant impact of negativity is on our physical health. Studies have shown that chronic stress and anxiety can lead to a range of health problems, including heart disease, high blood pressure, and digestive problems. Negative thinking can also impact our sleep, leading to insomnia and other sleep disorders, which can further impact our physical and emotional well-being.

Negativity can also impact our mental well-being, making it difficult to concentrate and make decisions. Negative thinking can lead to cognitive distortions, such as black-and-white thinking, overgeneralization, and catastrophizing, which can make it difficult to see the world in a balanced and nuanced way. This can lead to feelings of hopelessness and helplessness, which can further fuel negative thinking patterns.

Fortunately, there are strategies that we can use to overcome negative thinking patterns and cultivate a more positive mindset. One of the most effective strategies is to challenge negative self-talk by asking ourselves questions such as, "Is this thought realistic?" "What evidence do I have to support this thought?" "What would I tell a friend in this situation?" By questioning negative thoughts, we can begin to see the world in a more balanced and nuanced way, which can lead to greater emotional well-being.

Another strategy for overcoming negativity is to practice mindfulness and self-compassion. Mindfulness involves paying attention to the present moment without judgment, which can help us to let go of negative thoughts and emotions. Self-compassion involves treating ourselves with kindness and understanding, even when we make mistakes or face challenges. By practicing self-compassion, we can cultivate a more positive and supportive mindset, which can help us to overcome negativity and achieve greater overall well-being.

Therefore, negativity can have a significant impact on our lives, affecting our emotional, physical, and mental well-being. However, by practicing strategies such as challenging negative self-talk, mindfulness, and self-compassion, we can overcome negative thinking patterns and cultivate a more positive mindset. By doing so, we can improve our relationships, work, and overall quality of life, and achieve greater happiness and fulfillment.

The benefits of embracing positivity

Embracing positivity can have a transformative impact on our lives, affecting our emotional, physical, and mental well-being. When we choose to focus on the positive aspects of our lives, we can experience a range of benefits, including improved relationships, increased productivity, and greater overall well-being.

In this article, we will explore the benefits of embracing positivity and provide some strategies for cultivating a more positive mindset.

One of the most significant benefits of embracing positivity is on our emotional well-being. By focusing on the positive aspects of our lives, we can experience feelings of joy, gratitude, and contentment, which can help us to feel happier and more fulfilled. Embracing positivity can also lead to greater self-esteem and self-confidence, as we begin to believe in our abilities and strengths.

Another significant benefit of embracing positivity is on our relationships with others. By focusing on the positive aspects of others, we can build stronger, more meaningful connections with those around us. When we approach others with empathy, compassion, and kindness, we can foster a sense of trust and understanding, which can lead to greater intimacy and connection.

Embracing positivity can also have a significant impact on our work and productivity. When we approach our work with a positive mindset, we can be more creative, focused, and motivated. Positivity can help us to overcome challenges and obstacles, leading to greater innovation and success.

Positivity can also have a transformative impact on our physical health. Studies have shown that positive emotions can lead to lower levels of stress and anxiety, which can reduce the risk of a range of health problems, including heart disease, high blood pressure, and depression. Positivity can also lead to better sleep, which can further improve our physical and emotional well-being.

Fortunately, there are strategies that we can use to cultivate a more positive mindset and embrace positivity in our lives. One effective strategy is to practice gratitude by focusing on the positive aspects of our lives and expressing appreciation for them. This can help us to shift our perspective towards the good in our lives, leading to greater overall well-being.

Another strategy is to surround ourselves with positive influences, such as supportive friends and family members, uplifting media, and positive role models. By surrounding ourselves with positivity, we can create an environment that supports our well-being and reinforces our positive mindset.
Finally, practicing self-care can also help us to embrace positivity in our lives. By taking care of our physical and emotional needs, such as getting enough sleep, eating a healthy diet, and engaging in regular exercise, we can improve our overall well-being and cultivate a more positive mindset.

Hence, embracing positivity can have a transformative impact on our lives, affecting our emotional, physical, and mental well-being. By focusing on the positive aspects of our lives, building strong relationships with others, and approaching our work with a positive mindset, we can experience a range of benefits, including greater happiness, productivity, and overall well-being. By practicing strategies such as gratitude, surrounding ourselves with positivity, and practicing self-care, we can cultivate a more positive mindset and achieve greater happiness and fulfillment in our lives.

Understanding Negativity

Robert, a successful businessman had a great job, a loving family, and a beautiful home. However, despite all of his blessings, Robert often felt overwhelmed and unhappy.

Robert found himself constantly complaining about his job, his co-workers, and even his family. He would often snap at his loved ones, leaving them feeling hurt and confused. His negative attitude began to take a toll on his relationships, and he found himself becoming increasingly isolated and unhappy.

One day, a close friend of Robert's suggested that he attend a seminar on positive thinking. Robert was initially skeptical, but he decided to give it a try. During the seminar, Robert learned about the power of negativity and how it can impact our thoughts, feelings, and behaviors.

As Robert listened to the speaker, he began to realize how much his negative thinking was affecting his life. He realized that his negative thoughts were not only holding him back from experiencing true happiness, but they were also impacting those around him.

Robert decided to make a change. He began to practice positive thinking and gratitude, focusing on the good things in his life rather than the negative. He also started to surround himself with positive people who uplifted and encouraged him.

Over time, Robert noticed a significant shift in his mood and outlook on life. He began to feel more optimistic and hopeful, and his relationships improved. He found that he had more energy and enthusiasm for the things he loved to do, and he was able to approach challenges with a more positive mindset.

Looking back, Robert realized that his negative thinking had been a habit that he had fallen into overtime. But by attending the seminar and understanding the impact of negativity on his life, he was able to break free from that cycle and embrace a more positive, fulfilling life.

Negativity is a state of mind that is characterized by negative thoughts, emotions, and behaviors. It can manifest in a variety of ways, including pessimism, self-doubt, anxiety, anger, and depression. When we experience negativity, it can have a profound impact on our lives, affecting our relationships, health, and overall well-being.

One of the key aspects of understanding negativity is recognizing the role that our thoughts play in shaping our experiences. Negative thoughts can be self-perpetuating, creating a cycle of negativity that can be difficult to break. For example, if we constantly tell ourselves that we are not good enough, we may start to believe it and feel discouraged from pursuing our goals. Similarly, if we always focus on the worst-case scenario, we may feel anxious and overwhelmed, even if the situation is not actually as dire as we imagine it to be.

Another important aspect of understanding negativity is recognizing that it is often a result of external factors, such as stress, trauma, or difficult life circumstances. For example, if we experience a major life change, such as the loss of a job or a loved one, we may feel a sense of hopelessness and despair. Similarly, if we are constantly exposed to negative news or social media, it can be difficult to maintain a positive outlook on life.

However, it is important to remember that while external factors can contribute to negativity, they do not determine our emotional state. We have the power to choose how we respond to difficult situations and to reframe our thoughts in a more positive light. This requires practice and patience, as well as a willingness to challenge our negative beliefs and replace them with more empowering ones.

Overall, understanding negativity is an important step towards cultivating a more positive mindset. By recognizing the role that our thoughts and external factors play in shaping our experiences, we can take proactive steps to shift our mindset and overcome negativity.

The psychology of negative thinking

John, a successful businessman who struggled with chronic anxiety and pessimism.

Despite his many accomplishments, John was plagued by negative thoughts and feelings of inadequacy. He was constantly worrying about the future and catastrophizing potential outcomes. He also had a tendency to focus on his weaknesses and mistakes, rather than his strengths and successes.

John's negative mindset impacted his behavior in numerous ways. He was constantly second-guessing himself, procrastinating, and avoiding risks. He also had difficulty forming close relationships, as he was convinced that people would inevitably disappoint or reject him.

John eventually sought therapy to address his anxiety and negative thinking patterns. Through therapy, he was able to understand the root causes of his negative mindset and develop strategies to challenge and reframe his negative thoughts.

He learned to identify and question his automatic negative thoughts, recognizing that they were often based on faulty assumptions or cognitive distortions. He also practiced mindfulness techniques to increase his awareness of the present moment and cultivate a sense of inner calm.

Over time, John's mindset began to shift. He became more optimistic and confident, taking on new challenges and pursuing his goals with greater enthusiasm. He also developed closer relationships with family and friends, realizing that vulnerability and connection were key components of a fulfilling life.

John's story demonstrates the power of negative thinking to impact our emotions and behaviors. Left unchecked, negative thoughts can create a self-fulfilling cycle of anxiety and pessimism, limiting our potential and preventing us from experiencing joy and connection. However, by understanding the psychology of negative thinking and developing strategies to challenge and reframe our thoughts, we can break free from this cycle and cultivate a more positive, fulfilling life.

Negative thinking is a common phenomenon that many people experience at some point in their lives. Whether it's worrying about the future, dwelling on past mistakes, or feeling inadequate in the present, negative thinking can be a major source of stress and anxiety. Understanding the psychology of negative thinking can help us better understand why it happens and how we can work to overcome it.

One of the key factors that contribute to negative thinking is our cognitive biases. These biases are automatic thought patterns that influence our perception of the world around us. For example, confirmation bias is the tendency to seek out information that confirms our existing beliefs, while ignoring evidence that contradicts them. This can lead us to perceive the world in a more negative light, as we are more likely to focus on negative information that confirms our negative beliefs, rather than seeking out positive information.

Another important factor that contributes to negative thinking is our underlying beliefs and values. These beliefs are often shaped by our early experiences and can be deeply ingrained in our psyche. For example, if we grew up in an environment where we were constantly criticized or made to feel inadequate, we may develop a belief that we are not good enough, which can manifest as negative thinking.

In addition, our environment and social context can also play a role in negative thinking. For example, if we are constantly exposed to negative news or social media, it can be difficult to maintain a positive outlook on life. Similarly, if we are surrounded by people who are constantly negative or critical, it can be difficult to maintain a positive mindset.

Finally, negative thinking can also be a result of underlying mental health conditions, such as depression or anxiety. These conditions can affect the way we think and perceive the world, making it more difficult to maintain a positive mindset.

Overall, the psychology of negative thinking is complex and multifaceted. It can be influenced by a range of factors, including cognitive biases, underlying beliefs and values, environment and social context, and underlying mental health conditions. By understanding these factors, we can work to identify and overcome our negative thinking patterns, and cultivate a more positive mindset. This may involve challenging our negative beliefs, reframing our thoughts in a more positive light, and seeking out positive experiences and relationships that support our well-being.

Identifying negative thought patterns

Identifying negative thought patterns is an essential step in overcoming negative thinking and developing a more positive mindset. Negative thought patterns can be so ingrained in our thinking that they may not even be immediately apparent to us. However, by learning to recognize them, we can begin to challenge and replace them with more positive and constructive thoughts.

One common negative thought pattern is catastrophizing, which involves imagining the worst possible outcome of a situation. For example, if a person is running late for a meeting, they may catastrophize by imagining that they will be fired or that the meeting will be a disaster. This type of thinking can lead to feelings of anxiety and overwhelm, and can also make it difficult to take effective action to address the situation. Another negative thought pattern is all-or-nothing thinking, which involves seeing situations in black-and-white terms. For example, a person may believe that if they don't succeed at a task, they are a total failure. This type of thinking can be extremely limiting, as it prevents us from seeing the nuances and complexities of situations.

Self-blame is another common negative thought pattern, which involves blaming oneself for negative events or outcomes. For example, a person may blame themselves for a failed relationship or for not getting a job they applied for. This type of thinking can be damaging to self-esteem and can make it difficult to move forward and learn from past experiences.

Overgeneralization is another negative thought pattern, which involves making sweeping conclusions based on one or a few negative experiences. For example, a person who experiences rejection in one area of their life may conclude that they are unlovable or that they will never succeed in any area. This type of thinking can be self-fulfilling, as it can lead to a lack of effort and motivation to try new things or pursue goals.

Finally, personalization is a negative thought pattern that involves taking responsibility for events or outcomes that are outside of our control. For example, a person may feel responsible for a friend's bad mood, even though they have no control over the friend's emotions. This type of thinking can be exhausting and can lead to feelings of guilt and shame.

By learning to identify these and other negative thought patterns, we can begin to challenge them and replace them with more positive and constructive thoughts. This may involve reframing negative thoughts in a more positive light, seeking out evidence that contradicts negative beliefs, and practicing self-compassion and self-care. It may also involve seeking out support from friends, family, or mental health professionals to help us break out of negative thought patterns and cultivate a more positive mindset.

Therefore, identifying negative thought patterns is an essential step in overcoming negative thinking and developing a more positive mindset. By recognizing and challenging these patterns, we can begin to replace them with more positive and constructive thoughts, and cultivate greater resilience, well-being, and happiness in our lives.

The effects of negativity on our emotions and behaviors

Kaveri, a high school student who struggled with low self-esteem and a negative outlook on life.

Kaveri had always been a sensitive and introspective person, but as she entered high school, her negative thoughts and emotions began to take a toll on her. She constantly compared herself to others and felt like she didn't measure up. This led to feelings of anxiety, depression, and a lack of motivation.

Kaveri's negative mindset also impacted her behavior. She became withdrawn and isolated, avoiding social situations and even skipping school. She also began to engage in self-destructive behaviors, such as binge-eating and cutting.

Kaveri's parents became increasingly concerned about their daughter's mental health and reached out to a counselor for help. Through counseling, Kaveri was able to gain insight into the negative thought patterns that were fueling her emotions and behaviors.

She learned that her negative self-talk was based on false beliefs and comparisons that were not rooted in reality. She also learned coping strategies, such as positive self-talk, mindfulness, and self-compassion, that helped her manage her emotions and shift her mindset.

Over time, Kaveri's outlook on life began to change. She began to see herself in a more positive light and developed a sense of self-worth. She also started to engage in healthier behaviors, such as exercise and creative pursuits.

Kaveri's story highlights the profound impact that negativity can have on our emotions and behaviors. Left unchecked, negative thoughts and emotions can lead to a downward spiral of self-destructive behaviors and mental health issues. However, with the right support and tools, it is possible to break free from negative patterns and cultivate a more positive, fulfilling life.

Negativity can have a profound impact on our emotions and behaviors, often leading to a range of negative outcomes. Here are some of the ways in which negativity can affect us:

Decreased Motivation: Negativity can also lead to decreased motivation. When we focus on the negative aspects of a situation, it can be difficult to find the motivation to take action. This can lead to feelings of apathy and a lack of interest in activities that we once enjoyed.

Depression and Anxiety: Negative thoughts and emotions can lead to the development of depression and anxiety. When we constantly focus on negative events or situations, it can be difficult to see the positive aspects of life.

This can lead to a sense of hopelessness and a feeling of being overwhelmed.

Physical Symptoms: Negativity can also have physical symptoms. For example, people who are constantly negative may experience headaches, stomach aches, or other physical symptoms as a result of the stress and anxiety that negativity can cause.

Social Isolation: Negativity can also lead to social isolation. When we are constantly negative, it can be difficult to connect with others. This can lead to feelings of loneliness and a sense of being disconnected from the world.

Self-Sabotage: Negativity can also lead to self-sabotage. When we are constantly negative, it can be difficult to believe in ourselves or our abilities. This can lead to a lack of effort, a lack of motivation, and a lack of confidence.

Negative Relationships: Negativity can also lead to negative relationships. When we are constantly negative, it can be difficult to maintain positive relationships with others. This can lead to conflicts, misunderstandings, and a breakdown in communication.

Poor Decision-Making: Negativity can also lead to poor decision-making. When we are constantly negative, it can be difficult to make clear and rational decisions. This can lead to impulsive behavior, poor judgment, and a lack of foresight.

In short, negativity can have a significant impact on our emotions and behaviors. By recognizing the ways in which negativity affects us, we can begin to take steps to counteract its negative effects. This may involve practicing mindfulness, engaging in positive self-talk, and seeking out support from friends, family, or mental health professionals. With the right tools and support, we can learn to overcome negativity and cultivate a more positive mindset, leading to greater resilience, well-being, and happiness in our lives.

The Power of Positive Thinking

Nick Vujicic, a man born without arms or legs who has inspired millions with his positive attitude and determination.

As a child, Nick struggled with feelings of isolation and despair. He was bullied and often felt like an outcast. However, he eventually realized that he had the power to choose his own perspective and attitude towards life. Instead of dwelling on his limitations, he focused on his strengths and what he could do. He learned to swim, play golf, and even surf. He became a motivational speaker, sharing his message of hope and positivity with others.

Through his speeches, Nick has encouraged countless individuals to overcome their own obstacles and embrace a positive mindset. He has shown that even in the face of great adversity, it is possible to find happiness and fulfillment. His message is one of resilience, determination, and the power of the human spirit.

Nick's story is a powerful reminder that positive thinking can truly change the course of our lives. It allows us to focus on the good, even in difficult situations, and to approach challenges with a can-do attitude. Positive thinking can help us build resilience, cultivate healthy relationships, and increase our overall sense of well-being.

While it can be difficult to maintain a positive mindset all the time, Nick's story is proof that it is possible. By practicing gratitude, surrounding ourselves with supportive people, and focusing on our strengths, we can learn to see the world in a more positive light. By doing so, we can unlock the power of positive thinking in our own lives and achieve our goals and dreams.

Zamperini was an Olympic runner who became a prisoner of war during World War

II after his plane crashed into the Pacific Ocean. He and two other survivors floated in a life raft for 47 days before being captured by the Japanese.

During his time in the prison camp, Zamperini endured incredible physical and emotional abuse. He was beaten, starved, and tortured, and he witnessed the deaths of many of his fellow prisoners. But through it all, he maintained a positive attitude and refused to give up hope.

Zamperini used his skills as a runner to stay mentally strong. He imagined himself running free, and he visualized himself winning races. He also found ways to keep his mind occupied, such as by memorizing passages from the Bible and reciting them to himself.

Eventually, Zamperini was liberated from the prison camp, but his struggles were far from over. He returned home to a hero's welcome but struggled with post-traumatic stress disorder (PTSD) and turned to alcohol to cope. However, he eventually found his way back to a positive mindset and became a motivational speaker, sharing his story of perseverance with audiences around the world.

Zamperini's story is a testament to the power of positive thinking. Despite facing unimaginable hardships, he refused to give up hope and maintained a positive attitude. By doing so, he was able to endure and eventually overcome his struggles. His story serves as an inspiration to anyone who is facing adversity and struggling to stay positive.

Positive thinking is a powerful tool that can have a transformative impact on our lives. It involves adopting an optimistic outlook and focusing on the positive aspects of a situation, rather than dwelling on the negative. The power of positive thinking lies in its ability to shift our mindset, allowing us to approach challenges with greater resilience, creativity, and confidence.

Studies have shown that people who practice positive thinking tend to have better physical and mental health outcomes. They are less prone to stress, anxiety, and depression, and may even have stronger immune systems and lower rates of chronic illness. Positive thinking can also improve our relationships, as it allows us to approach others with greater kindness, empathy, and understanding.

One of the key benefits of positive thinking is its ability to increase our motivation and goal-setting abilities. When we adopt a positive mindset, we are more likely to see opportunities for growth and development, and to pursue our goals with greater determination and persistence. This can be especially powerful in the face of adversity, as a positive outlook can help us to stay focused and motivated even in the most challenging circumstances.

Another way in which positive thinking can impact our lives is through its effect on our self-esteem and confidence. When we believe in ourselves and our abilities, we are more likely to take risks, try new things, and pursue our passions. Positive thinking can help us to overcome feelings of self-doubt and imposter syndrome, allowing us to step into our full potential and achieve our dreams.

However, it's important to note that positive thinking does not mean ignoring or denying the challenges and obstacles we face in life. Rather, it involves approaching these challenges with a proactive, solutions-focused mindset. When we encounter difficulties, we can choose to focus on the opportunities for growth and learning that they present, rather than becoming discouraged or overwhelmed.

Ultimately, the power of positive thinking lies in its ability to shape our mindset and perspective, allowing us to approach life with greater resilience, creativity, and joy. By adopting a positive outlook, we can unlock our full potential and create a life that is filled with purpose, meaning, and fulfillment.

The science behind positive thinking

Positive thinking is not just a feel-good philosophy; it is supported by scientific research that demonstrates its benefits. Positive thinking has been shown to impact our brain function, behavior, and overall well-being.

One of the key ways in which positive thinking impacts our brain is through its effect on neurotransmitters. Neurotransmitters are chemicals that transmit signals between neurons in the brain, and they play a critical role in regulating our mood and emotions. Positive thinking has been shown to increase the production of neurotransmitters such as dopamine, serotonin, and endorphins, which are associated with feelings of happiness, pleasure, and well-being.

In addition to its impact on neurotransmitters, positive thinking has been shown to have a beneficial effect on our stress response system. Chronic stress has been linked to a wide range of negative health outcomes, including cardiovascular disease, diabetes, and depression. Positive thinking has been shown to help reduce stress by promoting the release of stress-reducing hormones such as cortisol and oxytocin, as well as by reducing inflammation and improving immune function.

Positive thinking has also been shown to impact our behavior and decision-making. When we approach situations with a positive outlook, we are more likely to engage in behaviors that support our goals and aspirations. Positive thinking has been linked to greater resilience, creativity, and problem-solving abilities, which can be especially helpful in challenging or uncertain circumstances.

Furthermore, positive thinking has been shown to have a powerful impact on our relationships. When we approach others with a positive, compassionate mindset, we are more likely to build strong, supportive relationships based on trust and mutual respect. Positive thinking can also help us to navigate conflicts and disagreements in a constructive, respectful way, which can lead to stronger, more fulfilling relationships.

Overall, the science behind positive thinking suggests that it is a powerful tool for improving our physical and mental health, enhancing our decision-making and problem-solving abilities, and strengthening our relationships. By adopting a positive mindset, we can create a life that is filled with meaning, purpose, and joy.

The benefits of positive thinking for our health and well-being

Positive thinking has been shown to have a powerful impact on our health and well-being. Research has demonstrated that people with a positive outlook on life tend to have better physical and mental health outcomes than those with a negative outlook. In this article, we will explore some of the benefits of positive thinking for our health and well-being.

Increased resilience: Resilience is the ability to bounce back from adversity. People with a positive outlook on life tend to be more resilient, as they are better able to see challenges as opportunities for growth and learning. This can help to protect us from the negative effects of stress and adversity.

Reduced stress and anxiety: One of the most well-known benefits of positive thinking is its ability to reduce stress and anxiety. When we approach life with a positive outlook, we are better able to manage the challenges that come our way. This can help to reduce feelings of stress and anxiety, which can have a negative impact on both our physical and mental health.

Improved immune function: Studies have shown that positive thinking can have a positive impact on our immune system. This is because positive emotions have been shown to stimulate the production of immune-boosting hormones such as oxytocin and serotonin. Additionally, positive thinking has been linked to improved sleep quality, which is essential for maintaining a healthy immune system.

Better cardiovascular health: Positive thinking has been linked to better cardiovascular health. This is because positive emotions have been shown to reduce inflammation and improve blood flow. Additionally, people with a positive outlook on life tend to engage in healthier behaviors, such as exercise and a healthy diet, which can further improve cardiovascular health.

Enhanced relationships: Positive thinking can have a positive impact on our relationships with others. When we approach life with a positive outlook, we are more likely to engage in positive interactions with others. This can help to strengthen our relationships, improve our social support, and increase our overall sense of well-being.

Improved self-esteem: People with a positive outlook on life tend to have higher levels of self-esteem. This is because they are better able to focus on their strengths and accomplishments, rather than dwelling on their weaknesses and failures. This can help to boost our confidence and improve our overall sense of self-worth.

Increased happiness: Perhaps the most obvious benefit of positive thinking is increased happiness. When we approach life with a positive outlook, we are more likely to experience positive emotions such as joy, gratitude, and contentment. This can help to improve our overall quality of life and increase our overall sense of well-being.

Therefore, positive thinking has a wide range of benefits for our health and well-being. By cultivating a positive mindset, we can reduce stress and anxiety, improve our immune function, increase our resilience, enhance our relationships, improve our self-esteem, and increase our overall sense of happiness and well-being. Whether we are facing challenges in our personal or professional lives, approaching life with a positive outlook can help us to navigate these challenges with greater ease and resilience.

Techniques for cultivating a positive mindset

Cultivating a positive mindset is not always easy, but it is an important practice for improving our mental and emotional well-being. Here are some techniques that can help us develop a more positive outlook on life:

Practice gratitude: Practicing gratitude involves focusing on the good things in our lives and expressing gratitude for them. This can involve keeping a gratitude journal, where we write down three things we are grateful for each day, or simply taking a few moments each day to reflect on the things we appreciate.

Reframe negative thoughts: Reframing involves looking at a situation from a different perspective, one that is more positive and empowering. For example, instead of thinking "I can't do this," we can reframe it as "I'm learning how to do this."

Practice mindfulness: Mindfulness involves being present in the moment and observing our thoughts and emotions without judgment. By practicing mindfulness, we can become more aware of our negative thought patterns and learn to let go of them.

Visualize success: Visualization involves imagining ourselves succeeding in our goals and aspirations. This can help us feel more confident and motivated to take action towards our goals.

Surround ourselves with positivity: Surrounding ourselves with positive people and environments can help us stay motivated and inspired. This can involve joining a supportive community, reading positive books and articles, or simply spending time in nature.

Focus on solutions, not problems: When faced with a problem, it can be easy to get stuck in a negative mindset. Instead, we can focus on finding solutions and taking action towards our goals.

Practice self-compassion: Self-compassion involves treating ourselves with kindness and understanding, especially during difficult times. This can involve practicing self-care, such as getting enough sleep and exercise, and speaking to ourselves in a kind and supportive way.

Engage in positive self-talk: Positive self-talk involves speaking to ourselves in a positive and empowering way. This can involve using affirmations, such as "I am capable and strong," or simply reframing negative self-talk into a more positive statement.

Practice forgiveness: Forgiveness involves letting go of anger and resentment towards ourselves and others. By practicing forgiveness, we can free ourselves from negative emotions and move forward with a more positive mindset.

Find meaning and purpose: Finding meaning and purpose in our lives can help us stay motivated and inspired. This can involve pursuing our passions, volunteering, or simply finding ways to make a positive impact on the world.

Overall, cultivating a positive mindset takes time and practice, but it is a worthwhile endeavor. By incorporating these techniques into our daily lives, we can improve our mental and emotional well-being, strengthen our relationships, and create a more fulfilling life.

Overcoming Negativity

Michael Jordan is considered one of the greatest basketball players of all time. However, his journey to success was not an easy one. In high school, he was cut from the basketball team due to his short stature. This was a huge blow to his confidence and he started to doubt his abilities. Despite this setback, Jordan was determined to become a great basketball player and began to practice even harder.

In college, Jordan faced another setback when he didn't make the US Olympic basketball team. This was a devastating blow for him, but instead of giving up, he used it as motivation to become better. He went back to his team and led them to a national championship.

Despite these successes, Jordan faced even more setbacks in his professional career. He faced constant criticism and negative comments from the media and other players. However, Jordan didn't let this negativity get to him. He used it as fuel to work even harder and prove his doubters wrong.

Eventually, Jordan led the Chicago Bulls to six NBA championships and became one of the most iconic athletes of all time. His perseverance, determination, and ability to overcome negativity are an inspiration to all of us.

J.K. Rowling, the author of the famous Harry Potter series. Before Rowling became a renowned author, she faced a series of setbacks and challenges that could have easily left her feeling defeated and negative.

In her early 20s, Rowling experienced a great deal of personal loss and was diagnosed with clinical depression. She lost her mother to multiple sclerosis and went through a difficult divorce. She also found herself a single mother, struggling to make ends meet on welfare benefits.

Despite these challenges, Rowling refused to give up on her dream of becoming a writer. She continued to work on her writing every chance she got, often writing in cafes while her baby daughter slept beside her.

Rowling also credits her experience with depression as a catalyst for her creativity. She said, "Depression gave me a gift...The idea for Harry Potter formed in my mind on a train journey from Manchester to London."

Rowling faced many rejections from publishers before finally finding success with Harry Potter and the Philosopher's Stone. However, even after the book was published, Rowling continued to face negative feedback and criticism.

Despite this, she persisted and continued to write the rest of the series, eventually becoming one of the most successful authors in history. Her story is a testament to the power of perseverance, resilience, and positivity in the face of adversity.

Rowling's journey also highlights the importance of having a growth mindset and reframing negative thoughts. She could have easily given up on her dream of becoming a writer after facing rejection and criticism, but she chose to see these setbacks as opportunities to learn and grow.

Overall, Jordon and Rowling's story is a reminder that setbacks and challenges are a natural part of life, but we have the power to overcome negativity and rise above our circumstances. By cultivating a positive mindset, practicing resilience and optimism, and reframing negative thoughts, we too can overcome adversity and achieve our goals.

Overcoming negativity can be a difficult task, but it is an important one if we want to lead happy and fulfilling lives. Negativity can come from a variety of sources, including our own thoughts and beliefs, as well as the people and situations around us. Whatever the source, negativity can hold us back and prevent us from reaching our full potential.

The first step in overcoming negativity is to recognize it for what it is. We may not always be aware of our negative thoughts and beliefs, but they can have a powerful impact on our emotions and behaviors. For example, if we constantly tell ourselves that we are not good enough, we may feel anxious and insecure, and we may avoid taking risks or pursuing our goals.

Once we have identified our negative patterns of thinking and behaving, we can begin to challenge and replace them with more positive ones. This can involve reframing our thoughts and beliefs, focusing on the present moment, and finding ways to cultivate positive emotions and experiences.

One technique for overcoming negativity is mindfulness, which involves paying attention to our thoughts and feelings without judgment. By becoming more aware of our negative thoughts and beliefs, we can learn to observe them without getting caught up in them. This can help us to gain a more balanced perspective and reduce our emotional reactivity.

Another technique is cognitive restructuring, which involves identifying and challenging our negative thoughts and beliefs. For example, if we believe that we will never be successful, we can challenge that belief by looking for evidence to the contrary, such as times when we have achieved success in the past.

Positive self-talk is another powerful tool for overcoming negativity. By using positive affirmations and statements, we can counteract our negative self-talk and cultivate a more positive mindset. For example, if we catch ourselves thinking, "I can't do this," we can replace that thought with, "I am capable of handling this challenge."

Ultimately, overcoming negativity requires a commitment to changing our thoughts and behaviors. It may not happen overnight, but with practice and perseverance, we can learn to cultivate a more positive mindset and overcome the obstacles that stand in our way. By doing so, we can live happier, more fulfilling lives and achieve our goals and dreams.

Strategies for challenging negative self-talk

Negative self-talk is an all-too-common experience for many people. We all have moments where we doubt ourselves, criticize ourselves, and put ourselves down. Unfortunately, these negative self-talk patterns can impact our self-esteem, our motivation, and even our physical health. The good news is that it is possible to challenge and change negative self-talk patterns. Here are some strategies for doing so:

Recognize when negative self-talk is happening: The first step in challenging negative self-talk is to become more aware of when it is happening. Notice when you are putting yourself down or thinking negative thoughts. You may want to keep a journal or make a mental note of when these thoughts occur.

Challenge negative thoughts: Once you have recognized negative self-talk, it's time to challenge those thoughts. Ask yourself if these thoughts are really true, or if they are based on assumptions or past experiences that don't reflect your current reality. Consider what evidence you have to support these thoughts, and whether there is any evidence that contradicts them.

Reframe negative thoughts: Once you have challenged negative thoughts, it's time to reframe them in a more positive way. Instead of thinking "I'm not good enough," for example, you might reframe that thought as "I am capable of handling this situation." You can also use positive affirmations to help reframe your thoughts. Repeat statements like "I am worthy" or "I am deserving of love and respect" to yourself.

Practice self-compassion: Negative self-talk can often stem from a lack of self-compassion. When you make a mistake or face a challenge, it's important to treat yourself with kindness and understanding. Imagine how you would talk to a friend who was going through a similar situation, and try to extend that same level of compassion to yourself.

Focus on the positive: When negative self-talk starts to creep in, try to focus on the positive aspects of the situation. Consider what you have accomplished in the past, and how those accomplishments can help you overcome your current challenge. Look for the good in yourself and the world around you.

Surround yourself with positivity: Sometimes, the people and situations around us can fuel our negative self-talk. Surround yourself with positive, supportive people who will lift you up and encourage you to be your best self. Seek out positive experiences and activities that bring you joy and fulfillment.

Practice mindfulness: Mindfulness can be a powerful tool for challenging negative self-talk. By becoming more aware of your thoughts and feelings, you can learn to observe them without getting caught up in them. This can help you to gain a more balanced perspective and reduce your emotional reactivity.

Challenging negative self-talk is not always easy, but it is a worthwhile endeavor. By becoming more aware of your thoughts and feelings, challenging negative thoughts, and reframing them in a more positive way, you can cultivate a more positive mindset and improve your overall well-being. Remember, you are worthy, deserving, and capable of achieving your goals and dreams.

Building resilience and optimism

Building resilience and optimism are crucial components in cultivating a positive mindset. Resilience refers to the ability to adapt and recover from adversity or stress, while optimism is the tendency to view situations in a positive light. By building these qualities, individuals can learn to approach challenges with a more positive outlook and better cope with setbacks.

One strategy for building resilience and optimism is practicing gratitude. Gratitude involves recognizing and appreciating the good things in life, no matter how small they may be. Research has shown that regularly practicing gratitude can improve well-being, increase resilience, and reduce symptoms of depression and anxiety. One way to practice gratitude is to keep a gratitude journal, where individuals write down things they are grateful for each day.

Another strategy is to focus on positive self-talk. Negative self-talk can be damaging and may contribute to feelings of low self-esteem and hopelessness. By consciously replacing negative thoughts with positive affirmations, individuals can train their minds to focus on the positive. For example, instead of thinking "I can't do this," individuals can replace it with "I can do this, I have the skills and abilities to succeed."

Mindfulness is also an effective technique for building resilience and optimism. Mindfulness involves paying attention to the present moment, without judgment. By practicing mindfulness, individuals can learn to regulate their emotions and respond to stress in a more positive way. This can help build resilience and optimism, as individuals become more aware of their thoughts and feelings and learn to respond to them in a more constructive manner.

Additionally, developing a growth mindset can help individuals build resilience and optimism. A growth mindset is the belief that intelligence and abilities can be developed through hard work and dedication. By embracing challenges and viewing failures as opportunities for growth, individuals can cultivate a more positive outlook and build resilience. Rather than feeling defeated by setbacks, individuals with a growth mindset view them as a chance to learn and improve.

Finally, building strong relationships with others can also contribute to resilience and optimism. Social support has been shown to be a key factor in promoting well-being and can help individuals cope with stress and adversity. By cultivating meaningful connections with others, individuals can build a support system that can help them navigate difficult times and stay positive.

In conclusion, building resilience and optimism are important components in cultivating a positive mindset. By practicing gratitude, focusing on positive self-talk, practicing mindfulness, developing a growth mindset, and building strong relationships, individuals can learn to approach challenges with a more positive outlook and better cope with setbacks. These strategies can help individuals build resilience and optimism, leading to greater well-being and a more positive outlook on life.

Coping with setbacks and failures

In life, setbacks and failures are inevitable. No matter how much effort we put into achieving our goals, things don't always go as planned. It can be a challenging and stressful experience, but it's important to learn how to cope with setbacks and failures in a healthy and positive way. By doing so, we can build resilience and develop the optimism we need to keep moving forward.

One strategy for coping with setbacks and failures is to practice self-compassion. This involves treating yourself with kindness and understanding, just as you would a good friend. Instead of beating yourself up over a failure, remind yourself that it's a normal part of the learning process. Give yourself permission to feel upset, but also remember that it's not a reflection of your worth as a person.

Another way to cope with setbacks and failures is to reframe your thinking. Instead of viewing a failure as a personal flaw, try to see it as a learning opportunity. Reflect on what went wrong and what you can do differently next time. Focus on the positive aspects of the situation, such as the lessons you learned or the progress you made, rather than dwelling on the negative.

It's also important to practice self-care during times of stress and difficulty. Make sure you're getting enough sleep, eating a healthy diet, and engaging in activities that bring you joy and relaxation. Taking care of yourself physically and emotionally can help you build the resilience you need to bounce back from setbacks and failures.

Finally, it can be helpful to seek support from others during challenging times. Talk to a trusted friend or family member about what you're going through. They may be able to offer a fresh perspective or provide emotional support. You could also consider seeking professional help from a therapist or counselor, who can provide guidance and support as you navigate the challenges of setbacks and failures.

Coping with setbacks and failures can be a difficult process, but it's also an opportunity for growth and learning. By practicing self-compassion, reframing your thinking, practicing self-care, and seeking support from others, you can build resilience and develop the optimism you need to keep moving forward in your life. Remember that setbacks and failures are a normal part of the human experience, and that with time and effort, you can overcome them and achieve your goals.

Embracing Happiness

Despite facing many setbacks and challenges in his life, the legendary basketball player Kobe Bryant maintained a positive outlook and found happiness in his love for the game.

Throughout his career, Kobe faced numerous injuries and setbacks that could have easily discouraged him. However, he used these setbacks as opportunities to learn and grow, always maintaining a positive attitude and a dedication to improving himself.

After retiring from basketball, Kobe found happiness in new endeavors such as writing and film production, which allowed him to explore different aspects of his creativity. He also devoted much of his time to his family, cherishing every moment he spent with them and sharing his love of basketball with his daughter, Gianna.

Tragically, Kobe and Gianna passed away in a helicopter crash in 2020. Despite this devastating loss, Kobe's legacy of positivity and love for life continue to inspire people around the world.

Kobe's story serves as a reminder that happiness is not just about achieving success or reaching certain goals, but also about finding joy in the journey and embracing the present moment. By maintaining a positive mindset and finding happiness in the things we love, we can live fulfilling and meaningful lives.

Jane had a successful career, a loving husband, and two beautiful children. Despite all of her blessings, Jane often found herself feeling unhappy and unfulfilled. She struggled with anxiety and depression and felt like something was missing in her life.

One day, Jane's best friend recommended that she attend a weekend retreat focused on mindfulness and self-discovery. Jane was hesitant at first, but she decided to take the plunge and sign up for the retreat.

During the retreat, Jane learned about the importance of gratitude and mindfulness in promoting happiness. She practiced meditation and journaling, and started to focus on the positive aspects of her life rather than dwelling on negative thoughts and feelings.

Jane also participated in group activities and connected with other attendees who were on their own paths of self-discovery. She realized the importance of positive relationships and social support in finding happiness and fulfillment.

As the weekend went on, Jane started to feel a sense of purpose and direction that she had been missing for so long. She identified her values and passions, and started to set goals for herself that aligned with those values.

When Jane returned home from the retreat, she made a conscious effort to continue practicing mindfulness and gratitude in her daily life. She also started to prioritize her relationships and social connections, and found that spending quality time with loved ones brought her immense joy and fulfillment.

Over time, Jane's overall outlook on life shifted. She felt more optimistic and resilient, and was better equipped to cope with the inevitable challenges and setbacks that came her way.

Jane's journey towards embracing happiness was not an easy one, but it was ultimately worth it. Through mindfulness, gratitude, and meaningful connections with others, she was able to find a sense of purpose and fulfillment that she had been searching for.

Embracing happiness is a mindset shift that can have a profound impact on our lives. It involves cultivating positive emotions, fostering gratitude, and focusing on the present moment.

Many of us live our lives striving for success, thinking that once we achieve certain goals, we will finally be happy. However, this mindset can be a trap that keeps us stuck in a cycle of always wanting more, without ever truly experiencing happiness.

Instead, embracing happiness involves recognizing that happiness is not something that can be achieved through external circumstances, but rather a state of mind that can be cultivated through intentional practices.

One key aspect of embracing happiness is cultivating positive emotions. This involves intentionally focusing on positive experiences and emotions, such as joy, gratitude, and contentment. By actively seeking out and savoring positive experiences, we can train our brains to focus more on the positive aspects of our lives, rather than dwelling on negative experiences or emotions.

Another aspect of embracing happiness is fostering gratitude. This involves consciously acknowledging and appreciating the good things in our lives, such as our relationships, our health, and the opportunities we have. By focusing on gratitude, we can shift our attention away from what we don't have, and instead focus on what we do have.

Finally, embracing happiness involves focusing on the present moment. Too often, we get caught up in regrets about the past or worries about the future. By focusing on the present moment and fully engaging in our experiences, we can cultivate a sense of presence and contentment that can contribute to our overall happiness.

There are many strategies that can be used to cultivate happiness, such as meditation, journaling, and engaging in activities that bring us joy. By incorporating these practices into our daily lives, we can begin to shift our mindset and embrace happiness as a way of life.

Research has shown that embracing happiness has a number of benefits for our health and well-being. For example, studies have found that people who are happier are more resilient in the face of adversity, have stronger immune systems, and are less likely to experience depression and anxiety.

In addition, embracing happiness can also have positive effects on our relationships. When we are happier, we are more likely to be kind, compassionate, and empathetic towards others. This can strengthen our relationships and help us to build more meaningful connections with others.

Ultimately, embracing happiness is a choice that we can make at any time. By cultivating positive emotions, fostering gratitude, and focusing on the present moment, we can shift our mindset and embrace happiness as a way of life. This can have a profound impact on our health, our relationships, and our overall sense of well-being.

The role of gratitude and mindfulness in promoting happiness

Shawn Achor, a Harvard-trained researcher and positive psychology expert had struggled with depression and negative thinking for much of his life, but after experiencing some personal setbacks, he began to explore the science of happiness and the power of positive psychology.

In his research, Achor found that gratitude and mindfulness were two key factors in promoting happiness and well-being. He developed a simple gratitude exercise that involved writing down three things he was grateful for each day, and encouraging others to do the same.

As he continued to practice gratitude and mindfulness, Achor noticed a significant shift in his own mood and outlook on life. He became more resilient and optimistic, and was able to overcome many of the negative thought patterns that had held him back in the past.

Achor's work has since become widely recognized in the field of positive psychology, and his TED Talk on "The Happy Secret to Better Work" has been viewed millions of times. Through his research and personal experience, Achor has demonstrated the powerful impact that gratitude and mindfulness can have on our lives, and the importance of cultivating a positive mindset for happiness and well-being.

Gratitude and mindfulness are two practices that can help us embrace happiness in our lives. These practices can help shift our focus from the negative aspects of our lives to the positive ones. By cultivating gratitude and mindfulness, we can develop a more positive outlook and experience greater happiness and well-being.

Gratitude is the practice of acknowledging and appreciating the good things in our lives. This can be anything from the people we love to the simple pleasures we enjoy. By focusing on the positive aspects of our lives, we can cultivate a sense of appreciation and joy. Gratitude has been shown to have a number of positive effects on our mental and physical health, including reducing stress, improving sleep, and increasing feelings of well-being.

One way to practice gratitude is to keep a gratitude journal. This involves writing down three to five things you are grateful for each day. This can be anything from a good cup of coffee to a supportive friend. By making a habit of focusing on the positive things in your life, you can shift your mindset from one of negativity to one of positivity.

Mindfulness is another practice that can help us embrace happiness. Mindfulness is the practice of being fully present in the moment, without judgment. By focusing on the present moment, we can let go of worries about the past or future and experience a greater sense of peace and happiness.

One way to practice mindfulness is through meditation. This involves sitting quietly and focusing on your breath or a mantra. As thoughts arise, you simply acknowledge them and return your focus to your breath or mantra. Over time, this practice can help you develop greater awareness of your thoughts and feelings, which can help you become more present and focused in your daily life.

Another way to practice mindfulness is through mindful breathing. This involves taking a few deep breaths and focusing your attention on your breath as it moves in and out of your body. This can help you become more aware of your body and your surroundings, and can help you feel more grounded and centered.

By cultivating gratitude and mindfulness, we can learn to embrace happiness in our lives. These practices can help us develop a more positive outlook and experience greater well-being and fulfillment. So, take a few moments each day to focus on the good things in your life and be present in the moment. Your mind and body will thank you for it.

Cultivating positive relationships and social support

The importance of social support and positive relationships in our lives cannot be overstated. Research has shown that people who have strong social connections tend to be happier, healthier, and more resilient in the face of stress and adversity. Positive relationships can provide emotional support, practical help, and a sense of belonging that can help us navigate life's challenges.

Cultivating positive relationships and social support can be an important part of embracing happiness. Here are some ways to do so:

Prioritize social connections: Make an effort to maintain and strengthen your relationships with family, friends, and colleagues. Reach out to people regularly, and make time for social activities.

Be a good listener: When you are interacting with others, focus on listening to what they have to say. Show empathy and understanding, and validate their feelings. This can help to strengthen your relationship and create a deeper sense of connection.

Practice kindness and generosity: Doing kind things for others can not only make them feel good, but can also increase your own happiness. Acts of kindness and generosity can help to build positive relationships and foster a sense of community.

Join groups and clubs: Participating in social groups and clubs can be a great way to meet new people and develop new interests. Look for groups that align with your hobbies or interests, or consider volunteering for a cause you care about.

Seek professional help: If you are struggling with mental health issues or other challenges that are impacting your ability to form positive relationships, seeking professional help can be a valuable step. Therapists and counselors can provide support, guidance, and strategies for improving your relationships and social connections.

In addition to social support, practicing gratitude and mindfulness can also be powerful tools for promoting happiness. Here's why:

Gratitude: Practicing gratitude involves focusing on the positive things in your life and expressing appreciation for them. Research has shown that regularly practicing gratitude can increase positive emotions, improve relationships, and boost overall well-being.

Mindfulness: Mindfulness involves paying attention to the present moment without judgment. It can help to reduce stress, improve mood, and increase resilience. Mindfulness can also help you to become more aware of your thoughts and emotions, and to respond to them in a more positive and constructive way.

Here are some strategies for cultivating gratitude and mindfulness:

Keep a gratitude journal: Take a few minutes each day to write down things you are grateful for. This can help to shift your focus from negative thoughts to positive ones.

Practice meditation: Meditation is a form of mindfulness practice that involves focusing your attention on the present moment. Regular meditation can help to reduce stress, improve mood, and increase self-awareness.

Engage in mindful activities: Activities such as yoga, tai chi, and walking can be a form of mindfulness practice. Engaging in these activities can help to calm your mind and promote a sense of relaxation.

Practice self-compassion: Treat yourself with the same kindness and understanding that you would offer to a good friend. This can help to cultivate a positive attitude towards yourself and others.

Hence, building positive relationships and social support, as well as cultivating gratitude and mindfulness, can be important strategies for embracing happiness. By making an effort to prioritize social connections and practice gratitude and mindfulness, you can increase your overall well-being and improve your ability to cope with life's challenges.

Finding meaning and purpose in life

Finding meaning and purpose in life is a fundamental human need that has been studied and explored by philosophers, theologians, and psychologists alike. At its core, it is the search for a deeper understanding of one's self and one's place in the world, as well as the quest to make a meaningful impact on society and leave a lasting legacy.

Adam Braun was the founder of Pencils of Promise, a non-profit organization that builds schools and increases educational opportunities in developing countries. Before starting Pencils of Promise, Adam was working in finance and had achieved financial success but felt unfulfilled and lacking purpose in his life. He decided to take a trip around the world, during which he had a chance encounter with a young boy in India who asked him for a pencil. This encounter inspired him to start Pencils of Promise, with a mission to increase access to education for children in developing countries.

Through his work with Pencils of Promise, Adam found meaning and purpose in his life by helping others and making a positive impact in the world. He also discovered that by focusing on something larger than himself, he was able to experience greater happiness and fulfillment.

In an interview, Adam shared that finding purpose and meaning in his life through Pencils of Promise has helped him to appreciate the small things in life, be more mindful and present, and feel a sense of gratitude for the opportunities and experiences he has had.

This example demonstrates how finding meaning and purpose in life can bring greater happiness and fulfillment, as well as a deeper sense of appreciation for the present moment and the experiences we have in our lives.

Research has shown that individuals who have a sense of purpose in life are more likely to experience greater levels of happiness, resilience, and well-being. They are also less likely to experience symptoms of anxiety, depression, and other mental health conditions. Furthermore, having a sense of purpose has been linked to better physical health outcomes, including a reduced risk of heart disease and stroke.

There are many ways to find meaning and purpose in life, and they can be unique to each individual. Some may find purpose through their career, while others may find it through volunteer work or hobbies. Regardless of how one finds purpose, there are some general principles that can help guide individuals in their search.

One important factor is to cultivate self-awareness and reflection. This involves taking the time to understand one's values, strengths, and passions. Reflecting on these aspects of oneself can help individuals identify the areas in which they feel most fulfilled and energized.

Another key factor is to focus on others and contribute to something greater than oneself. This can involve helping others in one's personal life, such as family and friends, as well as contributing to larger social causes or movements. Giving back to others can be a powerful way to find meaning and purpose in life.

Additionally, finding meaning and purpose in life often involves taking risks and stepping outside one's comfort zone. This may involve trying new experiences, pursuing new goals, or facing fears and challenges. Embracing uncertainty and being open to new possibilities can help individuals discover new passions and opportunities for growth.

Finally, it is important to remember that finding meaning and purpose in life is an ongoing journey, rather than a destination. It may involve exploring different paths and making adjustments along the way. It may also involve seeking out support from others, such as friends, family, or mental health professionals.

In short, finding meaning and purpose in life is a complex and multifaceted process. It involves self-awareness, reflection, contribution to others, risk-taking, and ongoing exploration. By cultivating these factors and seeking out support when needed, individuals can discover a sense of fulfillment and well-being that can have a positive impact on all aspects of their lives.

Putting it into Practice

Serena Williams, considered one of the greatest tennis players of all time, has faced many challenges and setbacks throughout her career. However, she has always maintained a positive mindset and used it to her advantage.

One notable example of Serena's positive mindset was during the 2015 French Open. She was two games away from being eliminated in the second round when she injured her leg. Instead of giving up, Serena focused on the positive and used the injury as an opportunity to show her resilience. She fought through the pain and won the match in three sets, ultimately going on to win the tournament.

In an interview after the match, Serena talked about the importance of having a positive attitude. She said, "I always try to stay positive, no matter what. Even when things are tough, I try to focus on the good things and find a way to turn things around. I think that's what separates the great players from the good players."

Serena also uses positive affirmations and visualization techniques to help her stay focused and motivated. In her book "On the Line," she writes about how she visualizes herself winning each match before she steps onto the court. She also uses positive affirmations, such as "I am strong" and "I am powerful," to help her stay confident and focused during matches.

In addition to her positive mindset on the court, Serena is also known for her positive outlook off the court. She is an advocate for many causes, including equal pay for women and breast cancer awareness, and often uses her platform to spread positivity and inspire others.

Serena's story is a testament to the power of positivity and how it can help us overcome challenges and achieve our goals. By focusing on the positive, using positive affirmations and visualization techniques, and staying resilient in the face of setbacks, we can all cultivate a positive mindset and improve our happiness and success in life.

LeBron James, one of the greatest basketball players of all time has been known for his strong work ethic, positive attitude, and ability to lead his teams to victory.

Early in his career, James faced a lot of criticism and negativity from both fans and the media. However, he didn't let that discourage him. Instead, he used the negativity as motivation to work harder and prove his doubters wrong.

James also made a conscious effort to cultivate positive relationships and a strong support system. He surrounded himself with people who believed in him and encouraged him to stay positive, even during difficult times.

In addition, James is a strong believer in the power of visualization and positive self-talk. Before every game, he takes time to visualize himself making successful plays and winning the game. He also repeats positive affirmations to himself, such as "I am strong," "I am focused," and "I am confident."

Through his positive mindset and hard work, James has achieved tremendous success both on and off the court. He has won multiple NBA championships, Olympic gold medals, and numerous individual awards. He is also known for his philanthropic work and dedication to social justice causes.

James' story is a great example of how putting positivity into practice can help improve happiness and achieve success. By focusing on the positive, cultivating strong relationships, and using positive self-talk and visualization, we can overcome negativity and achieve our goals.

Jacinda Ardern, the Prime Minister of New Zealand has been praised for her empathetic leadership style, which emphasizes kindness and compassion. In the wake of the 2019 Christchurch mosque shootings, Ardern was widely praised for her response, which included wearing a hijab in solidarity with Muslim communities and emphasizing the need for love and unity. She also quickly implemented gun control measures in response to the attack.

Ardern has also implemented policies aimed at improving the well-being of New Zealanders. In 2019, her government released a "well-being budget," which prioritized funding for mental health services, child poverty reduction, and addressing climate change. She has also implemented policies aimed at reducing inequality, such as increasing the minimum wage and providing free school lunches for low-income students.

Ardern's leadership style and policies reflect a commitment to positivity and the belief that people can work together to create a better world. Her emphasis on empathy and compassion has helped to foster a sense of community and well-being in New Zealand. By putting positivity into practice in her leadership, Ardern has not only improved her own happiness, but the happiness of those around her.

One Hollywood actor who has spoken about the transformative power of positivity in his life is Dwayne "The Rock" Johnson. In an interview with Oprah Winfrey, he shared how he went through a difficult phase in his early 20s when he was cut from his football team, lost his girlfriend, and was battling depression.

Johnson turned to fitness and positive thinking to help him overcome these challenges. He started lifting weights and working out, and began to focus on his goals and dreams. He would write them down every day, and visualize himself achieving them. He also started practicing gratitude, focusing on the good things in his life and being thankful for them.

These habits helped Johnson develop a positive mindset, and he began to see improvements in his life. He went on to become a successful professional wrestler, and later transitioned to acting. He has starred in blockbuster movies such as the Fast and Furious franchise and Jumanji.

Johnson has also used his platform to promote positivity and kindness. He is known for his motivational posts on social media, where he encourages his followers to work hard, stay positive, and be kind to others. He has also started his own charitable foundation, the Dwayne Johnson Rock Foundation, which supports children and their families facing illness and hardship.

Johnson's story is a powerful example of how putting positivity into practice can lead to significant personal growth and success. By focusing on his goals, practicing gratitude, and staying positive, he was able to overcome adversity and achieve his dreams. His commitment to using his success to help others is a testament to the transformative power of positivity.

Luvly, a 35-year-old marketing executive who was going through a rough patch in her personal life. She was recently divorced, struggling to find a new sense of purpose and direction in life, and feeling generally unhappy and unfulfilled.

Luvly knew she needed to make a change, so she decided to embark on a journey of self-discovery and personal growth. She started by reading books and articles on positive psychology and happiness, and began practicing daily gratitude journaling and mindfulness meditation.

She also started to focus on building positive relationships and social connections in her life, making an effort to spend more time with family and friends and joining a local community group that aligned with her interests.

As she started to feel more positive and optimistic about life, Luvly decided to set some goals for herself to help give her a sense of direction and purpose. She started small, setting achievable goals like running a 5k race and learning a new hobby, and gradually worked her way up to more ambitious goals like starting her own business.

Throughout her journey, Luvly encountered setbacks and challenges, but she remained resilient and focused on the positive aspects of her life. She continued to practice gratitude, mindfulness, and self-compassion, and sought out support from her friends and family when she needed it.

Over time, Luvly's efforts paid off. She found herself feeling happier, more fulfilled, and more connected to herself and those around her. She was proud of the progress she had made and felt excited about the future.

These stories demonstrate the power of positivity and perseverance in the face of adversity. By cultivating a positive mindset and refusing to let setbacks define us, we can overcome challenges and achieve our goals.

Putting the principles of positivity and happiness into practice can be a challenging but rewarding process. It requires consistent effort and dedication to changing one's thoughts and behaviors, but the benefits are well worth it.

One effective way to start putting positivity into practice is to set small, achievable goals for oneself. These goals could be as simple as taking a few minutes each day to practice gratitude, or making an effort to be more present and mindful in one's daily activities.

By setting achievable goals and gradually building on them, individuals can begin to cultivate positive habits and mindsets that will contribute to their overall well-being.

Another important aspect of putting positivity into practice is seeking out social support and positive relationships. By surrounding oneself with people who uplift and inspire, individuals can create a supportive network that encourages positivity and growth. This may involve joining a social club or group, or simply reaching out to friends and family for support and encouragement.

Practicing self-care is also an important component of embracing happiness. This may involve engaging in regular exercise, eating a healthy and balanced diet, getting enough sleep, and taking time for oneself to relax and recharge. By prioritizing self-care, individuals can create a foundation of physical and emotional well-being that will support their efforts to cultivate positivity and happiness.

Finally, it's important to remember that putting positivity into practice is a process that requires patience and persistence. There will inevitably be setbacks and challenges along the way, but by staying committed to the goal of creating a more positive and fulfilling life, individuals can overcome these obstacles and continue to grow and thrive.

Ultimately, putting positivity into practice is about making a conscious decision to focus on the good in life, rather than dwelling on the negative. By cultivating positive habits, seeking out social support, and prioritizing self-care, individuals can create a life that is filled with happiness, meaning, and purpose.

Practical exercises and activities for developing a positive mindset

Developing a positive mindset requires practice, effort, and a commitment to change.

Here are some practical exercises and activities that can help in cultivating a positive outlook:

Gratitude journaling: Take some time each day to write down three things you are grateful for. This exercise helps to shift your focus to the positive aspects of your life and cultivates a sense of appreciation.

Mindfulness meditation: Practice mindfulness by focusing on your breath and being present in the moment. This exercise helps to reduce stress and anxiety, and increase self-awareness.

Visualization: Visualizing success can help to boost motivation and confidence. Take some time each day to visualize yourself achieving your goals and living the life you desire. This can help you stay motivated and focused on what you want to achieve.

Limit negative self-talk: Become aware of negative self-talk and replace it with positive affirmations. For example, instead of saying

"I can't do this," say "I am capable and will give it my best effort."

Surround yourself with positivity: Spend time with positive people, read uplifting books or articles, and listen to music that makes you feel good.

Gratitude journaling: Take a few minutes each day to write down three things you are grateful for. This helps shift your focus to the positive aspects of your life, and can improve your overall mood and well-being.

Positive affirmations: Choose a few positive statements that resonate with you. Examples might include "I am worthy of love and respect," or "I trust in my ability to overcome challenges." Repeat these affirmations throughout the day to yourself regularly, especially when you are feeling negative.

Mindful breathing: Take a few minutes to focus on your breath and bring your attention to the present moment. This can help calm your mind and reduce stress and anxiety.

Acts of kindness: Engage in small acts of kindness each day, such as holding the door open for someone or offering a compliment. This can help boost your mood and increase feelings of connection and well-being. Perform random acts of kindness, such as buying a coffee for a colleague or offering to help a neighbor. These acts can boost your mood and create positive connections with others.

Exercise: Engaging in regular exercise has been shown to improve mood and reduce symptoms of anxiety and depression. Find a form of exercise that you enjoy and make it a regular part of your routine. Exercise releases endorphins, which are feel-good hormones that can help to improve mood and reduce stress.

Spending time in nature: Spending time in nature has been shown to have a range of positive benefits, including reducing stress and improving mood. Take a walk in a park, hike in the woods, or simply spend time in your garden or a local green space.

These exercises and activities can help to develop a positive mindset and overcome negativity. It is important to remember that change takes time and effort, but with persistence and commitment, it is possible to cultivate a more positive outlook on life.

Creating a personalized plan for overcoming negativity and embracing happiness

Creating a personalized plan for overcoming negativity and embracing happiness can be a powerful tool for achieving lasting positive change in your life. By taking the time to reflect on your personal goals, values, and strengths, you can develop a plan that is tailored to your unique needs and circumstances.

Here are some steps you can take to create your own personalized plan for overcoming negativity and embracing happiness:

Identify your goals: Start by thinking about what you want to achieve in terms of your mindset and emotional well-being. Do you want to be more positive, optimistic, and resilient? Do you want to develop stronger relationships with others? Do you want to find more meaning and purpose in your life? Write down your goals in clear and specific terms.

Assess your current state: Take stock of your current mindset and emotional well-being. What are your strengths and weaknesses? What are the factors that contribute to your negative thinking or behaviors? What coping strategies have you used in the past that have been effective or ineffective?

Develop a plan of action: Based on your goals and assessment, develop a plan of action that includes specific strategies and activities that you will undertake to achieve your desired mindset and emotional well-being. This may include developing a daily gratitude practice, engaging in regular exercise or mindfulness meditation, seeking out social support, or engaging in therapy or coaching.

Create accountability and support: Share your plan with trusted friends, family members, or a therapist or coach. Ask for their support and encouragement, and consider setting up regular check-ins to assess your progress and make adjustments as needed.

Celebrate your successes: As you make progress toward your goals, celebrate your successes and acknowledge the hard work and effort that you have put in. This will help to reinforce your positive changes and motivate you to continue your journey toward a more positive and fulfilling life.

Remember, creating a personalized plan for overcoming negativity and embracing happiness is a process, and it may take time and effort to achieve your desired outcomes. Be patient, persistent, and compassionate with yourself, and keep your focus on your goals and the positive changes that you are working to achieve.

Action Points

The action points for the path to positivity can be summarized as follows:

(i)   Embrace a growth mindset: Believe in your ability to change and grow, and approach challenges as opportunities to learn and improve.

(ii)   Practice gratitude: Focus on the things you're thankful for in your life, and take time to appreciate them.

(iii)   Cultivate self-compassion: Be kind and understanding to yourself, and don't beat yourself up over mistakes or setbacks.

(iv)   Practice mindfulness: Be present in the moment, and learn to observe your thoughts and emotions without judgment.

(v)   Surround yourself with positivity: Spend time with people who uplift and inspire you, and seek out activities that bring you joy and fulfillment.

(vi)   Set meaningful goals: Identify what truly matters to you, and set goals that align with your values and aspirations.

(vii) Take action: Break down your goals into actionable steps, and take consistent, deliberate action towards achieving them.

(viii) Embrace failure: Recognize that failure is a natural part of the learning process, and use it as an opportunity to grow and improve.

(ix)   Practice resilience: Develop the skills and mindset to bounce back from setbacks and adversity, and use challenges as opportunities for growth.

(x)   Practice self-care: Take care of your physical, emotional, and mental well-being by getting enough sleep, exercise, and healthy nutrition.

(xi)   Foster positive relationships: Invest in your relationships with family, friends, and colleagues, and work to resolve conflicts in a positive and constructive manner.

(xii) Let go of negative thoughts and emotions: Learn to recognize and release negative thoughts and emotions, and cultivate a more positive and compassionate inner dialogue.

(xiii) Practice forgiveness: Let go of resentment and grudges, and cultivate forgiveness for yourself and others.

(xiv) Seek out learning opportunities: Embrace opportunities for learning and growth, and challenge yourself to try new things and expand your horizons.

(xv) Focus on the present moment: Cultivate mindfulness and focus on the present moment, rather than worrying about the past or future.

By incorporating these additional action points into your daily life, you can continue to strengthen your positivity and resilience, and build a life filled with happiness, meaning, and purpose.

Conclusion

The path to positivity is a journey that we must embark upon if we want to live a fulfilling and happy life. It is not always easy, and there will be obstacles along the way, but with determination and the right mindset, we can overcome anything. The power of positivity is immense, and it can transform our lives in ways we never thought possible.

As we continue on this path, let us remember the words of Maya Angelou, who said, "I can be changed by what happens to me. But I refuse to be reduced by it." Life is full of challenges, but it is up to us to choose how we respond to them. We can either let them bring us down, or we can use them as opportunities to grow and become stronger.

Throughout this book, we have explored various strategies for developing a positive mindset, including challenging negative self-talk, building resilience and optimism, coping with setbacks and failures, and finding meaning and purpose in life. We have also learned about the role of gratitude, mindfulness, positive relationships, and social support in promoting happiness.

While it can be challenging to maintain a positive outlook all the time, the benefits of doing so are undeniable. By continuing to practice the exercises and techniques outlined in this book, we can create a personalized plan for overcoming negativity and embracing happiness.

It is important to remember that this is a journey, and there may be setbacks along the way. However, with persistence and dedication, we can continue on the path to positivity and transform our lives for the better. We encourage you to continue to practice the techniques outlined in this book and to seek out additional resources and support as needed.

The power of positivity lies within each of us, and it is up to us to choose to embrace it. By doing so, we can create a life filled with joy, meaning, and fulfillment.

As I conclude this book, "The Path to Positivity," I want to share my own experience in the path of positivity. When I was younger, I struggled with negative thoughts and self-doubt. I often felt like I wasn't good enough and didn't deserve success or happiness. This mindset held me back from pursuing my dreams and achieving my goals.

But over time, I began to realize the power of positivity in transforming my life. Through reading books, attending seminars, and listening great people, I learned to challenge my negative thoughts and replace them with positive affirmations. I started to believe in myself and my abilities, and as a result, I began to achieve my goals and experience more happiness and fulfillment in my life.

I know firsthand that the journey to positivity isn't always easy. It takes time, effort, and dedication to change your mindset and habits. But I also know that it's worth it. When we embrace positivity, we open ourselves up to a world of possibilities and abundance. We attract more positivity and happiness into our lives, and we become more resilient in the face of adversity.

So I encourage all of you to continue on the path to positivity. Take the lessons and exercises from this book and apply them to your life. Believe in yourself and your ability to create a positive, fulfilling life. And remember, even when setbacks and challenges arise, you have the power to choose a positive mindset and overcome negativity.

In the words of Tony Robbins, *"Beliefs have the power to create and the power to destroy. Human beings have the awesome ability to take any experience of their lives and create a meaning that disempowers them or one that can literally save their lives."*

So let us choose to create a positive meaning in our lives and use it to empower us. Let us continue on the path to positivity, knowing that the journey may be challenging, but the rewards are worth it.

Gratitude

To my better half, whose unwavering support and well wishes have been the driving force behind the creation of yet another book on success, this work is gratefully dedicated.